# NAVIGATING AMBIGUITY

# NAVIGATING AMBIGUITY

## Creating Opportunity in a World of Unknowns

Andrea Small & Kelly Schmutte
Paper artwork by Reina Takahashi
Photographs by Andria Lo

TEN SPEED PRESS
California | New York

HASSO PLATTNER
Institute of Design at Stanford

# Contents

"It's a confusing time."

—John Waters

# A Note from the d.school

At the Stanford d.school, *design* is a verb. It's an attitude to embody and a way to work. The core of that work is trying, to the best of one's abilities, to help things run more smoothly, delight more people, and ease more suffering. This holds true for you, too—whether design is your profession or simply a mindset you bring to life.

Founded in 2005 as a home for wayward thinkers, the d.school was a place where independent-minded people could gather, try out ideas, and make change. A lot has shifted in the decade or so since, but that original exuberant and resourceful attitude is as present today as it was then.

Our series of guides is here to offer you the same inventiveness, insight, optimism, and perseverance that we champion at the d.school. Like a good tour guide, these handbooks will help you find your way through unknown territory and introduce you to some fundamental ideas that we hope will become cornerstones in your creative foundation.

Use data to tell stories with *The Secret Language of Maps*. Overcome everything between you and doing work that matters in *Drawing on Courage*. And in this book, move uncharted challenges to discover creative possibility.

It's time for *Navigating Ambiguity*!

love,
the d.school

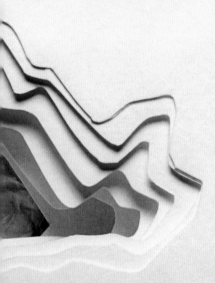

**Enter** Ambiguity

THE FU
HAS N
BEEN
UNCE

ITURE
EVER
MORE
TAIN.

"What fresh hell
will tomorrow bring?"

—Liz Lemon

**We live in a time of rapidly changing contexts.**

Deadly global pandemics, tightening immigration, catastrophic job loss, persistent racism and discrimination, increasing average temperatures, economic instability and volatility, diminishing trust in leaders and media, increasing frequency and severity of weather events, mounting pressure on global food and water security, expanding terror threats, rising ocean temperatures, falling fertility rates, growing food intolerances and allergies, worsening political polarization, evaporating retirement funds, murder hornets, increasing competition for scarce natural resources, robots taking jobs, plastics filling the oceans, mounting evidence tying social media to depression, ongoing animal habitat loss and degradation, acidifying oceans, widespread misinformation, people still refusing to wear masks, dwindling arts funding, a growing sense of powerlessness, stagnating incomes, today's music ain't got the same soul, widespread stress and anxiety, polarization of high- and low-skilled employment, extinction threatening one

THE F
HAS N
BEEN
UNCEI

TURE

EVER

MORE

TAIN!

"The future is dark, which is the best thing the future can be, I think."

—Virginia Woolf

**We live in a time of rapidly changing contexts!**

Falling global child mortality rates, a growing global movement to end racism and systemic injustice, fewer people living in extreme poverty, the ozone hole decreasing, doubled global life expectancy, greater access to electricity and running water, widening adoption of sustainable environmental practices, plummeting illiteracy rates, unprecedented groundswells of citizen action against injustice, increasing attention on workplace equity and inclusion practices, landmark victories for LGBTQ+ rights, new technology fighting online abuse, increasing volunteerism among teenagers, Siberian tigers saved from extinction, decreasing cigarette sales, growing trust in medical scientists, live video streams of bears catching fish, improved disease identification through machine learning, declining numbers of stray animals and increasing pet adoption, the return of crewed spaceflights, positive strides in destigmatizing mental health, a growing second wave of the sharing economy, development of revolutionary new healthcare technologies, increasing receptivity to expanding social safety net programs, body positivity movements changing the fashion and beauty

# Change and uncertainty are the new normal.

Let's be honest. The world is complex and in flux. Massive changes are afoot, and not all of them are pleasant. Society is polarized and divided. Our relationships with institutions and the truth are changing. The economy is constantly fluctuating.

Change and uncertainty are normal parts of work and life, too. Our lives no longer follow a strictly linear path (if they ever did). Career transitions. Caregiving. Side hustles. Layoffs. Self-care. Gigging. Sound familiar? Where there once was one path, now there are many.

"The biggest challenge to businesses right now isn't uncertainty, but ambiguity—a condition in which the future is unclear, the past is no help, and we don't even know what we don't know."

—Alice Kogan and Sandeep Pahuja, design leaders

Even though cosmologists say we basically understand only about 4 percent of our universe, we still seem to think we should be able to control things and solve any and every problem in two shakes of a bunny's tail. It's hard to relish a lack of concrete solutions or see the opportunity in the unknown, but it might just be worth it.

This book isn't about the uncertainty running rampant in our lives. But it is about designing through its challenges.

# Ambiguity holds creative possibility.

Some things about our collective future and our personal future are uncertain (Will the tornado season be bad? Will Punxsutawney Phil see his shadow? Will my broken ankle heal in time for the race?), and many more things are unknown (How will humans respond to the climate crisis? What does the future of online learning and remote work look like? Can I really hack it as a designer?). Unlike things that are uncertain, ambiguous things are unformed and emergent—they could yet be created or interpreted in any number of ways. These are things that humans (you!) have the potential to shape. You can build the future (rather than try to predict it).

This unknown is where creativity and ambiguity live.

Difficult challenges in a complex, changing world require creativity to tackle, and ambiguity is a natural part of that creative work. You simply can't have one without the other.

David Kelley, cofounder of the d.school and founder of the global design and innovation company IDEO, says, "It's necessary to go to a place where you have this feeling that you don't know—the problem isn't defined well, you don't exactly know what direction you're going to go. . . . And it's scary, getting used to that, getting into a place where you're embracing that notion that 'I don't know' where this is going." But Kelley explains that this often uncomfortable rite of passage through the unknown is essential because you "have to be in this state in order to go to a place that's new to the world."

Do you need to think of yourself as a designer to read this book? Nope. Do we believe that thinking like a designer can offer you a new way to look at and engage with ambiguity? One hundred percent. In fact, we bet that, since you picked up this book, you can readily conjure an ambiguous demon you're wrestling right now. How did we know?!*

*Magic

# The ability to navigate ambiguity isn't locked inside a black box.

We're going to crack open the box and lay out what's inside for you, like ~~Pandora's box~~ a delicious chocolate egg with a toy inside. This is our opportunity to share with you what we have learned through our years of teaching at the d.school; running our own businesses; and working with a multitude of design agencies, nonprofits, start-ups, and corporations.

You'll learn to **understand ambiguity**—clarifying what the word even means, what happens in your brain when you experience it, and how every response is personal. The more you can learn to embrace ambiguity through both **acting** and **adapting**, the greater your ability to face the unknown with confidence will be.

Then we will shift to **navigating ambiguity**—figuring out how to move in, with, and through the unknown in a way that bolsters your creativity and emboldens your decision making. As you'll see, navigating ambiguity is a **balancing** act, not a formula.

Eventually, you will **emerge** with a new perspective and the creative ability to access and embrace ambiguity, if you so choose.

As you can see, it's not
all **black** and **white**.

Ambiguity is about the many **shades** of **gray** in between.

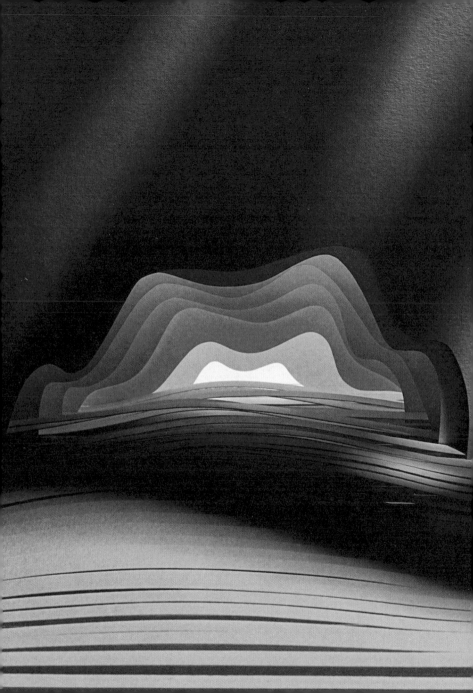

# Part I
# **Understand** Ambiguity

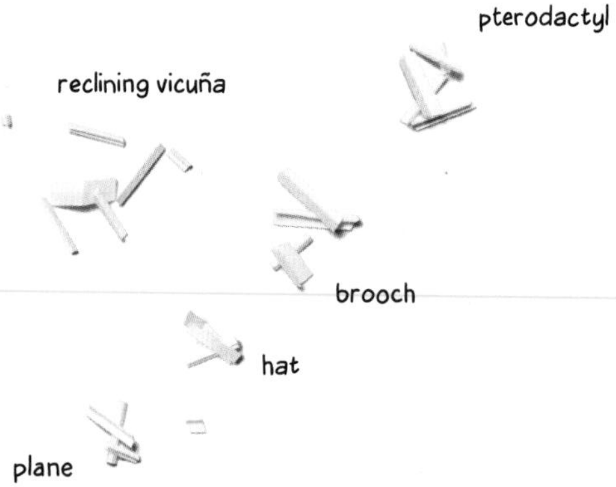

pterodactyl

reclining vicuña

brooch

hat

plane

# What Is Ambiguity?

The first step to understanding ambiguity is to *define* it, which is a delightfully existential challenge we've been pondering ourselves for several years. Let's attempt to disambiguate ambiguity, shall we?

am•bi•gu•i•ty
/ˌam-bə-ˈgyü-ə-tē/

According to "the internet," the definition of *ambiguity* is:

a: the quality or state of being ambiguous

b: something that can be understood in two or more possible ways

The word *ambiguity* comes from the Latin *ambiguus*, which was formed by combining *ambi-* meaning "both ways" and *-agere* meaning "to act." Ambiguity is about **holding two ideas at the same time** and understanding something in more than one way. It's about dualities, multiplicities, and active interpretation.

All cleared up? No? We're shocked.*

*We are not shocked.

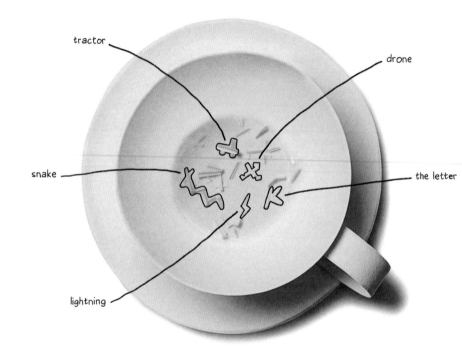

tractor

drone

snake

the letter

lightning

tea leaves

Tasseography is the practice of reading patterns in tea leaves (or coffee grounds or wine sediments) left in the bottom of a cup. You can "read" the tea leaves by allowing your imagination to play around with the shapes suggested in their arrangement. You might see a country, a heart, or a raven. Or read deeper . . . is that an apple? Or the Apple logo? Does it mean I need to limit my screen time? Am I reading too much tea?

Ambiguity is a layer of meaning people apply to perfectly unambiguous stuff. When you read the tea leaves at the bottom of the cup, the cup and dregs are not ambiguous. Ambiguity lies in the multiple meanings that you might derive from their arrangement. It emerges from the many ways you interpret reality. But before you settle on one interpretation, ambiguity gives you permission to be creative. As soon as you choose an interpretation, ambiguity naturally evaporates.

Our response to ambiguity—both our interpretations and our emotional response—is not objective. It's deeply connected to experience, context, history, and character. What you see might not be what anyone else sees. What you see today might be different tomorrow.

# Ambiguity ≠ uncertainty.

Ambiguity may contain uncertainty, but they're different. Dictionaries define *uncertainty* as something that is not clearly or precisely determined; something unknown, vague, indistinct, or subject to change. Uncertainty implies that there is something to be *certain* about. An absolute truth or fact exists. It's more black and white.

**Uncertainty might look like:**

- Why am I getting issues of *Domestic Rabbits* magazine?
- Will I get the job or not?
- What if the ferret hates the new rabbit?
- Will my rent check bounce?
- When will they respond to my email?
- Does this mole look normal?
- When will the quarantine end and my life go back to normal?
- Will life *ever* return to normal?

With ambiguity, on the other hand, there's no singular, correct answer. It allows for layers of meaning on anything. No absolute truth or fact exists. Your mind is free to explore—and to imagine possibilities that are unknown or don't currently exist.

**Ambiguity might look like:**

- What could this sheet of blank paper become?
- What can I learn from new contexts and cultures?
- What happens when I step outside of my comfort zone?
- What if I am neither thing? Or both?
- What happens when I allow contradictory data to exist?
- What are the different ways I can interpret something?
- How might I respond to fluctuating timelines or constraints?
- After months of starts and stops and highs and lows, what shape will ~~this book~~ "it" take?

In philosophy and art, ambiguity and uncertainty are decidedly different. In this book, we blur them together a bit because the words *uncertainty* and *ambiguity* are intertwined in our lexicon, and untangling semantics isn't our goal. In general, when we refer to ambiguity or uncertainty in this book, we mean holding multiple ideas or possibilities. We also say *not knowing, the unknown, the gray area,* or *the* _____ . For the purposes of this book, we break our own rules, we keep it vague, we keep you guessing. Some might say we practice what we preach.

Even if ambiguity and uncertainty are decidedly different on paper, they are not very different in the brain. Perhaps the terms intertwine because humans also intertwine their reactions. As you'll read, the brain often reacts to ambiguity as if it is uncertainty.

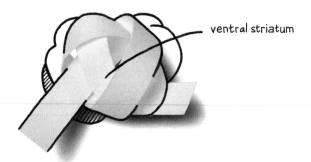

ventral striatum

# Brain Stuff

The A-word itself evokes associations with something being unsettled, unclear, and frustrating. Our brain tends toward the negative in that way. It's easier to think of the bad times than the good times (which is a bummer).

## What happens in our brains when we experience ambiguity?

Evolutionarily, the brain dislikes uncertainty, regarding it like a type of pain. The brain therefore tries to avoid uncertainty, and in its place creates story upon story to explain it away. The brain is so powerful it causes people to vividly imagine their way to closure. It's a foundation of creativity. Dr. Robert Burton, former chief of neurology at the University of California at San Francisco-Mt. Zion Hospital, said, "Only in the absence of certainty can we have open-mindedness, mental flexibility, and willingness to contemplate alternative ideas."

But certainty feels rewarding, like fitting in the last piece of a challenging puzzle. In 2009, researchers at the National Eye Institute showed that the brain responds to the possibility of finding new information in just the same way as it responds to other rewards like food and drink—with a little dopamine hit. Dr. Burton goes even further, saying, "certainty can approach the power of addiction." We gravitate toward certainty because it feels fabulous, and away from uncertainty because it feels . . . the opposite of fabulous.

In 2016, researchers at University College London ran a shocking little experiment measuring how uncertainty affects people. Research participants were asked to lift rocks in a video game. If a snake was under the rock, they received a nonvirtual, very real electric shock via an electrode on the back of their left hand. The participants' stress was tracked through physiological signs, like sweating and pupil dilation, and saying things like "please, no more, make it stop" (we're guessing).

The "game" was designed to keep participants fluctuating between confidence and uncertainty about what was under the rock.

This study uncovered a fundamental aspect of psychology: stress peaks when uncertainty peaks—when people were the most unsure about what was under the rock. It feels more stressful to be *uncertain* than it does to feel *certain about something bad*. We prefer to *know*, even if it's not good. For example, it can feel more stressful not knowing how a critique will go than knowing you're definitely about to get chewed out. Or not knowing whether you'll get the role or funding or project. The waiting game can feel more stressful than the potential bad outcome itself.

## The quest for certainty is a survival instinct.

Imagine it is 11,650 years ago. It's the end of the Ice Age, and the Earth is warming up. You're an early human, and you're approaching a dark cave. There might be a saber-tooth cat in there, *or* it might serve as a cool shelter. Your brain prioritizes the negative outcome (eaten by a saber-tooth cat) because

your life's on the line. "Our brains and bodies evolved to not die—evolution works from failure, not from success," says professor of neuroscience and author Dr. Beau Lotto. Our species would be long gone if we hadn't developed this little brain trick. But even though we've outlived the saber-tooth cats, a sense of uncertainty still generates a threat response in our limbic system.

This natural instinct to live is totally awesome. But it gives us a *bias toward certainty* and *away from uncertainty*. We have a natural tendency to prefer knowing over not knowing. The brain wants to make decisions based on the information it has and to complete the picture, even when it might be best to remain open.

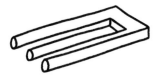

When the brain can't expeditiously complete the picture, we feel uneasy, lost, or anxious. Most people have a hard time admitting that they don't know. There's so much pressure

> "Filling in the blanks replaces the truth that we don't entirely know with the false sense that we do."
>
> —Rebecca Solnit

put on us to have all the answers. Worse still is when we don't even know if we're answering the right *question*. Compound this with the surrounding pressures of life and work, throw in some constraints like time and money, and ambiguity mutates into anxiety.

But premature closure leads to reducing the richness of complexity, drawing faulty conclusions, and over-simplifying problems. And that leads to sub-par, mundane ideas.

It's our job as designers to resist the chemical bias for certainty. Your brain naturally builds limiting beliefs about what is happening, and you must continually break through these ingrained beliefs to imagine something new. "And though that's not particularly comfortable," Patrice Martin, designer and former creative director at IDEO.org, says, "it allows us to open up creatively, to pursue lots of different ideas, and to arrive at unexpected solutions."

Navigating ambiguity is often thought of as a passive thing. *Just relax*, we are told. *Wait it out. Go with the flow. Let it be. Practice acceptance.*

However, navigating ambiguity takes work. It can be exhausting. Even when you think you're relaxing and letting it be, your brain is working in the background to solve unknowns and make connections. It's a muscle that can be built with patience and effort—not a hand-wavy, woo-woo, abstract thing that you do or don't have.

**Intolerance** for ambiguity
is characterized by*

**Tolerance** for ambiguity
is characterized by**

 Need for categorization

 No need for categorization

 Need for certainty

 Need for curiosity

 Inability to allow good and bad traits to exist simultaneously

 Encouragement of good and bad traits to exist simultaneously

 Acceptance of attitudes representing black-and-white life views

 Rejection of attitudes representing black-and-white life views

 A preference for familiar over unfamiliar

 A preference for unfamiliar over familiar

 Rejection of the unusual or different

 Celebration of the unusual or different

 Early selection and maintenance of one solution

 Generation and exploration of many ideas

 Premature closure

 Patience

* Bochner, Stephen. "Defining Intolerance of Ambiguity," *The Psychological Record*, 1965.

** According to your authors.

**Try this:**

"Ambiguity is like_____

because _____."

# Attitudes About Ambiguity

In 2017, we enlisted hundreds of our students in an experiment to understand how people relate to ambiguity. Before we get to the results, try it yourself. What metaphor best describes your relationship to ambiguity?

**Start by thinking of a recent time you experienced ambiguity or some unknown. This could have been a time when:**

- Your next steps were unclear.
- You faced more questions than answers.
- You recognized multiple pathways or possibilities.
- Your idea of a single right outcome was challenged.
- You wrestled with some existential challenge.
- You pondered ambiguity for too long.
- Your perception of the grand illusion was shattered.

Think back to that ambiguous time. How did you feel? How did you respond? Why?

Now, based on that experience, what metaphor captures your *attitude* about ambiguity or the unknown? It can be a simple metaphor or a conceptual, complex metaphor.

We tried this exercise with a large swath of our student body. Their metaphors were illuminating. We got some obvious ones, of course: fog, water, clouds. But many stretched our minds: toothpaste, mice, a jar (no bad ideas, et cetera). When we stepped back, we saw some interesting patterns emerge across their metaphors.

Some students saw ambiguity as being antagonistic—a *hurdle* between them and a goal. Or it felt like a fog— something that needed to be removed to allow them to see clearly. Their metaphors were about **enduring** ambiguity until it is over, like getting caught under an awning during a cloudburst while you're carrying a bunch of piñatas.

Other students with a little more practice (and a little more creative confidence) shared metaphors that described **engaging** with ambiguity—facing it head on, like skydiving or wandering alone in an unexplored forest. Here, ambiguity wasn't as antagonistic; it was simply unknown. There might be a thrill in taking a risk on an unfamiliar outcome, or an openness to seeing things a different way and letting an unexplored path take you where it may.

Still other students had a pretty seasoned take on ambiguity. Rather than seeing it as a momentary roadblock between moments of clarity, they **embraced** it as a field of opportunity, theirs to access at will. The metaphors here painted pictures of a richly and densely forested patch of rainforest, searching for gold at the beach, or falling in love.

We also noticed that students' relationships with ambiguity— and the way they navigate them—shifted with time, experience, and growth in design skills and abilities. New designers gravitated toward simply enduring ambiguity, while those with more design experience engaged or embraced it.

Endure

Engage

Embrace

# How do you respond to ambiguity?

## Endure

**Do you prioritize a defined conclusion? Do you push through ambiguity as fast as possible?**

Ambiguity is something that comes between you and a solution. It's antagonistic to your objective. It must be conquered or eliminated to reach a goal.

## Engage

**Do you dip in and out of ambiguity? Do you see it as an appealing challenge?**

Ambiguity is an off-road adventure, an alternate path to a goal. It might be rewarding and helpful or dangerous and detrimental. Its value is a chosen gamble. Exhilaration and exhaustion are equally expected.

## Embrace

**Do you rely on the existence of ambiguity? Do you thrive in the unknown?**

Ambiguity is oceanic and ever-present. Exploration is a challenge *and* an opportunity. The longer you spend in it, the more likely you are to discover something new. Every direction is a possibility. Navigation isn't simple. It requires patience and practice.

# Use these attitudes as:

### A common language and communication tool.

Go-to terms are useful. They give shape to experience. They help express struggles and break down intangible feelings. They can also help you compose teams with a balance of different approaches to ambiguity.

### A self-awareness diagnostic tool.

Use them to diagnose your relationship with ambiguity at any given moment. How do you approach navigating ambiguity? Do you see yourself gravitating to a particular attitude? You might generally gravitate toward one approach, but you might also feel differently in different contexts.

### A tool to see how your approach changes over time.

Transformation can happen with repeated complex problem-solving. While one navigation strategy might feel familiar or comfortable at a given time, strategies are context-dependent and always changing.

# What are your attitudes toward ambiguity?

## 1    Create a metaphor.

Start by thinking of a specific time you experienced ambiguity or some unknown. This could have been when:

- Your next steps were unclear.
- You recognized multiple pathways or possibilities.
- Your idea of a singular outcome was challenged.

Think back to that time. What were you feeling? How did you respond? Why?

Based on that memory, take a stab at crafting a metaphor statement that captures your relationship to ambiguity. You can use the fill-in-the-blank structure below as a guide. Have some fun with this, and try a couple on for size if you're feeling stuck.

Note: Your comparisons can be as expressive as you want them to be. Your metaphor might be very simple or conceptual—there are no right answers here!

Ambiguity is like...

[object, action, moment, place, anything]
_____

because...

[reason it resonates with you].
_____

## 2 Dig for meaning.

Now put on your detective hat. Answer the three questions below to help you decode the attitude(s) reflected in your metaphor. Where can you spot attitudes of enduring, engaging, or embracing ambiguity?

|  | **endure** ambiguity | **engage** ambiguity | **embrace** ambiguity |
|---|---|---|---|
| **How would you describe your ability to act in your metaphor?** | Ambiguity happens to me. | I can choose to take part in ambiguity. | Ambiguity is a tool and a resource. |
| **What does your metaphor say about your openness and adaptability?** | I need to get to certainty and find the "right" outcome. | I accept that there are many possible outcomes. | The more possible outcomes, the better. |
| **Does your metaphor include any of these elements?** | Feeling lost or disoriented, like seeking the exit of a maze<br><br>Overcoming a fear or challenge, like climbing to the top of a mountain<br><br>Wrestling with the "right" choice, like standing at a crossroads | Choosing or creating your own path, like swimming in the ocean<br><br>Taking the plunge, like paragliding<br><br>Sensing danger and excitement simultaneously, like watching a summer storm | Working to find something of great value, like making a scientific discovery<br><br>Actively making something better with time, like painting a blank canvas<br><br>Choosing to turn challenges into opportunities (like having too many zucchinis) |

## 3   Notice how "when" can change things.

Your attitude toward ambiguity might shift depending on the context. Use the grid to explore different past and present strategies for dealing with ambiguity (fill in what you can). It's valuable to notice when and why your attitude varies!

Remember, ambiguity is not about the black and white, but rather the gray space in between. There are no hard lines between attitudes, no fixed mindsets, and there's always room for interpretation and reinterpretation. If we've upped your self-awareness a notch, mission accomplished!

| What is/was your attitude . . . | endure ambiguity | engage ambiguity | embrace ambiguity |
|---|---|---|---|
| . . . on a recent or current work project? | | | ex: "I embraced ambiguity when offered the chance to teach a totally new and untested class format last year." |
| . . . in your personal life? | ex: "I tend to endure ambiguity when the commitment level in a relationship feels unknown." | | |
| . . . regarding your next career move? | | | |
| . . . ten years ago? | | ex: "Back then, starting a project before it was fully planned was my first step to engage with ambiguity" [patting self on back]. | |

"The key to survival is knowing you're lost."

—Unknown

# Embracing Ambiguity

Deep-sea divers start their explorations by mapping a matrix on the seabed. It helps them organize the unknown. They methodically inspect each square, one by one. If they come across a treasure chest in square 1A, they drop a pin and move on, exploring further. It's counterintuitive. They found something, maybe something valuable. They could stop. Shouldn't they stop!? They don't. There might be a whole sunken ship twenty squares away. Or a new species of disappointed-looking blobfish. Or they might not find anything else. But they are there to discover, and they trust that the treasure chest in the first square will be there when they get back.

Designers, like deep-sea divers and explorers, dive into the ocean of ambiguity because they see opportunity in the deep dark recesses of the possible. If you engage in ambiguity, in the realm of multiple right answers and unturned stones, you are rewarded by the exact thing you might have been afraid of—the unexpected.

# Ambiguity is at the core of human-centered design.

Human-centered design is a problem-solving process that focuses on creating solutions for people's real needs. When we start, we are immersed in not knowing . . . not knowing the solution, not knowing the answers, and sometimes not even knowing if you're barking up the right tree. Who are you solving for? What is the context? What do people want or need?

After a problem is defined, the questions continue as the focus shifts to solving the problem. What feels most pressing or exciting? What happens if you just try it? What can you do in the time you have? There are no "right" answers; there are infinite ways to interpret the problem and creatively respond. This is full-on ambiguity territory.

One of India's largest farmer-owned agriculture enterprises, RamRahim, hired designer and policy expert Raghav Raghunathan to find out why their farmers' produce was undervalued. His first challenge was to understand the problem thoroughly. Raghav spent a whole year listening to farmers and stakeholders and eventually learned that middlemen had come to control the cleaning, grading, and sorting of produce. This ultimately contributed to the devaluation of the product.

Together, Raghav and the farmers created a way to localize grading using a low-cost, gravity-fed seed grader that was easy to use and didn't require electricity (a key feature for remote, rural farmers). Through much iteration, this grass-roots solution was collectively adopted by the community and reduced the need for middlemen.

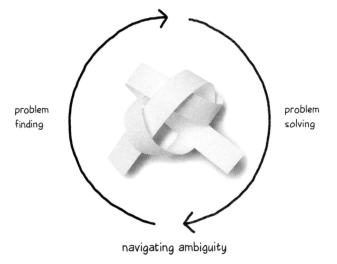

problem
finding

problem
solving

navigating ambiguity

If you're creating something new to the world, you will definitely have to wrestle with ambiguity at some point. Engaging ambiguity isn't a choice; it's inherent in the process of getting to any great outcome. How designers approach ambiguity is accessible to anyone.

Have you ever heard the phrase, "Don't be so solution-oriented" or "Don't rest on that first idea"? People can have a tendency to come in with their own "treasure chest," or idea, fearing that they're not going to find something else. Or, when the unknown feels too uncomfortable, they might rigidly cling to the first thing they find. The d.school's creative director Scott Doorley says, "Not only do we love to grab the first treasure we find, we'd even like to lug in our own treasure chest, drop it in the water, and pretend we found it there."

# What you discover might even alter your path.

The element of discovery in an ocean of ambiguity is twofold: there's the discovery itself (*what* you find on the ocean floor), and then there's the potential for that discovery to alter the arc of your work (*how* you move forward). Meaningful discoveries profoundly change the way you understand a problem or conceive of a solution. Designers call this reframing, or changing your point of view. Maybe your original goal or process no longer makes sense. Embracing ambiguity actually helps you find and evolve your path.

You can always come back to your early ideas, but try to stay open to the search. You might find something special in the next square. Or you might find nothing. But trust that it will certainly be something. Or nothing at all.

And that sure is something.

. . . or nothing.

## ll gray areas are created equal.

Navigating ambiguity helps us find our way through
difficult problems, but that is not the only way ambiguity
comes into play in creative work. While it's a designer's
job to challenge a bias for certainty, there are times when
you cannot and should not proceed without clarity—with
your team, organization, and partners.

## ery, uncertainty, and vagueness can be to manipulate and control.

Gaslighting, fake news, disinformation, alternative facts—
ambiguity can be wielded in a variety of ways, not just as
a means of positive creativity. It can be used to subvert
the power of others. Examples of this dark side are easy to
spot—like when people in positions of power (*ahem*—
politicians) use ambiguity to cloud the truth, confuse reality,
deflect attention, and delay decision making.

The ambiguity that we love as creative fuel is, for some, the
same ambiguity they can use to manipulate. It could look
innocent: a moving deadline, an unresolved issue, a loosely
worded email. But it leads to larger systemic problems—
and it can torment the individuals or groups it is put upon.
It might feel like something is vague or perpetually up in
the air—like that promotion or resolution is right there, you
just need to "prove yourself." Vagueness and misdirection

can keep people in turmoil looking for resolution, never knowing which way things will go, and often insinuating a consequence or imagining the worst. And in our world of "move fast and break things," not having a clear *no* is sometimes interpreted as a *yes*.

Getting comfortable with the unknown is *not* an antidote for bad communication, toxic culture, unreasonable timelines, and crushing workloads. Change and uncertainty are normal parts of every work environment, but some leaders and organizations might use "ambiguity" as an excuse to put people under more pressure, the implication being that *the fault lies with the employee* if they are "unable to cope with the ambiguity."

**You might recognize unhealthy ambiguity in your own work when:**

- Information is withheld.
- Decision making is unclear.
- Directives are chaotic or confusing.
- Timelines and boundaries are ignored.
- Fees and dates have been alluded to but not concretely set.
- Roles and responsibilities are unclear.
- Questions go unanswered.
- The finish line keeps moving.

If you're using ambiguity as a tool for creativity, yay! You're on the right track. If you're creating ambiguity for others (deliberately or not), stop it. We're on to you.

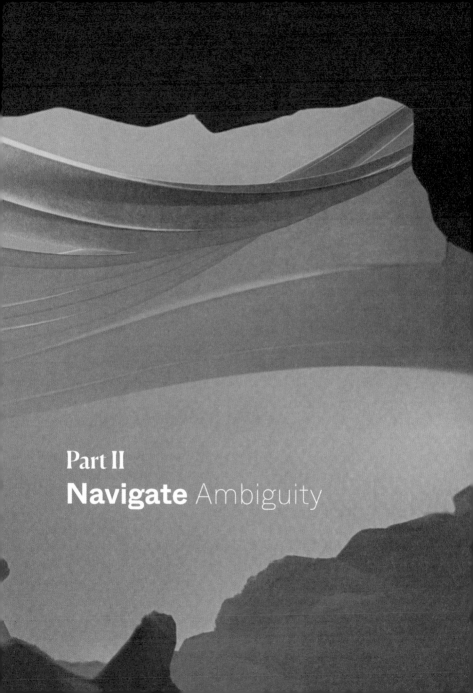

**Part II**
**Navigate** Ambiguity

# Navigation Tools

Before complex technology existed, navigators looked to the constant objects of the physical world—like the sun—to orient themselves. From the dawn of history to right this second, people use these predictable objects in the sky to determine time and direction. Even in space travel, astronauts use the sun in the same way ancient navigators did.

**Icelandic spar:** a colorless, transparent variety of calcite used by the Vikings to identify the sun's position, even while the sky was obstructed by foul weather

**Astrolabe:** an extremely cool-looking analog calculator that determines latitude by measuring the angle between the North Star and the horizon

**Cross-staff:** an ancient Mesopotamian device that uses a stick to measure the angle between the horizon and a celestial body but caused blindness when measuring against the sun

**Back-staff:** a device that does the same thing as the cross-staff, but with the user's back to the sun, avoiding risk of blindness

**Horn or whistle:** a sound-maker used to alert nearby vessels in difficult conditions, like fog or high traffic, or during emergencies, like running out of sunscreen

**Kamal:** an Arabian adaptation of the Polynesian latitude hook that uses a string and a piece of wood to make the measurements needed to calculate latitude

**Stars:** exploding balls of gas in the sky

**Human hand:** a conveniently attached appendage used to measure the angles between stars and the horizon

**Antikythera mechanism:** a machine made by the Greeks in the first century BCE to predict astronomical positions, which some say is the first computer

**Birds:** winged animals whose appearance at sea can be a sign of land beyond the horizon

"If you can identify the stars as they rise and set, and if you have memorized where they rise and set, you can find your direction."

—Nainoa Thompson, master navigator and president of the Polynesian Voyaging Society

If the Polynesian Triangle were a landmass, it would form the largest country on earth, with more than a thousand islands scattered across ten million square miles of the Pacific Ocean. For centuries, Polynesian navigators, called "wayfinders," have learned how to travel and live in this expansive space and call it home. Rather than using high-tech instruments, wayfinders explore and orient by recognizing important signs and patterns in the natural world—things like the position of specific stars, weather and climate, the migration patterns of various species, the ocean's currents, colors of the sea and sky, and cloud formations relative to landmass. Yep, you guessed it—this is *not* easy to do. Turning on your GPS seems tempting when confronted with the need to stay up most hours of the day and night, as the crew's master navigator must do, staying hyperattuned to your canoe's surroundings and carefully calibrating your direction in response.

Hawaiians, Micronesians, and many other peoples of Polynesia have practiced this noninstrument–based system of navigation for centuries, and thus have honed their ability to accurately voyage thousands of miles across open ocean. Master navigators have a highly evolved set of tools and mental frameworks for interpreting their environment and acting in the absence of information. They have a deep respect for the natural world and learn to adapt to the weather and other unexpected scenarios along the way by changing their original course.

Balancing purposeful vision with flexibility requires an intensely dynamic approach. Wayfinders are continually **acting** and **adapting**.

**Acting** is taking purposeful initiative in the face of the unknown.

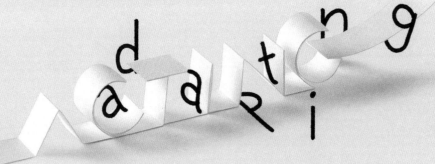

**Adapting** is flexing to changing conditions.

**Together,** they combine to help you, your team, or your organization **embrace ambiguity** and navigate it with confidence.

# Acting.

Grit, determination, autonomy, courage, perseverance, tenacity, nerve, resourcefulness, stamina

❮ You might identify with some of the these related characteristics

**Acting** requires making choices and not getting frozen by fear. It's working with what you do have even when you find yourself with limited control over a situation. It's a close cousin of agency, which economist Dr. Ronald Ferguson defines as "the capacity and propensity to take purposeful initiative—the opposite of helplessness."

**Acting** requires you to match your skills, resources, and knowledge with the problem at hand. It's based in the confidence generated by a powerful blend of past experience (knowing what's worked before) and honed craft (processes, tools, methods, techniques). You can actively *increase* your capacity to act with each new approach you learn and apply.

**Acting** doesn't always look the same. Sometimes it is straightforward—doing the work that needs to be done. Other times it's testing things out to make sure you're on the right track. Or it means stepping back to see how your work is unfolding. In every case, acting involves taking initiative.

The ability to act is deeply intertwined with power, privilege, and entrenched social structures. Everyone manages ambiguity, but circumstances often dictate that some people have more agency to act than others. There are systemic barriers that, historically and to this day, oppress some people more than others. These inequities affect how power and privilege are distributed. Recognizing these dynamics and your own biases at a deeper level is crucial in building your own—and others'—capacity to act with intention and responsibility.

As d.school designer and educator Louie Montoya explains, "The most 'design malpractice' happens when people are acting but not reflecting." Being action-oriented is only as valuable as your ability to reflect on those actions—internal reflective work is critical and cannot be divorced from taking action.

# Adapting.

**You might identify with some of the these related characteristics ❯**

Flexibility, responsiveness, resilience, receptivity, elasticity, fluidity, openness, humility

**Adapting** requires you to respond to shifting information, changing contexts, and pop-up shenanigans. When you're staying adaptable in the face of the unknown, you acknowledge new information and proactively **respond** accordingly, whether it's timelines, practices, or expectations.

Working in early-stage ventures or emerging industries, for example, requires a great deal of adaptability. Technologies and policies change daily, even hourly, requiring you to continually flex. Adapting can sometimes feel at odds with tangible goals and targets, but unless you adapt, you might never hit your target.

**Adapting** also means more than going where the wind and waves take you. It requires actively expanding and holding open the set of possibilities for where you're headed. It goes back to the root definition of ambiguity: being able to hold two ideas at the same time. If you can keep different pathways open in parallel, you're staying flexible. This might require letting go of specific outcomes to open yourself and your work to new directions.

When the COVID-19 pandemic hit in early 2020, theaters were shuttered overnight. American Ballet Theatre, a premier classical ballet company, adapted by commissioning new works in "ballet bubbles" (small groups of dancers that lived and worked together with the choreographer) to film and stream online. Dancers from ABT and beyond were inspired to use the extra time to offer free virtual classes, creating unprecedented public access to the rarified world of ballet.

Being adaptable means you value input outside yourself; you're not the only source for all brilliant ideas. An unwillingness to adapt can stem from a number of factors: tradition, poor communication, ego, fear of negative outcomes, momentum, investment, and more. Leading by example, you can also encourage those around you to value change instead of fearing it.

**Acting and adapting are behaviors that counterbalance and improve each other.**

When your abilities to act and to adapt are *both* low, you simply have to **endure** ambiguity—keep your nose down and tough it out. It's not ideal, but it's reality. As your abilities to act and to adapt increase, that's when you can **engage** and even **embrace** ambiguity.

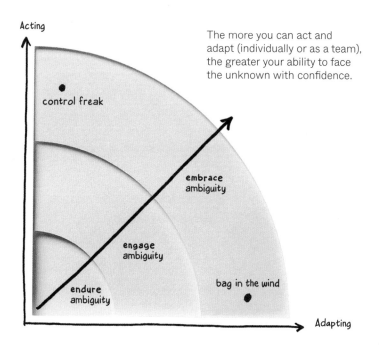

Acting

The more you can act and adapt (individually or as a team), the greater your ability to face the unknown with confidence.

control freak

embrace ambiguity

engage ambiguity

endure ambiguity

bag in the wind

Adapting

Acting and adapting aren't mutually exclusive, of course. Sometimes, one ability might be really low, so you have to compensate by increasing the other (this goes for individuals *and* teams).

If your ability to act is low, you need to be more adaptive. Office closed? School canceled? Everything going online? WiFi keeps crashing? Adapt, adapt, adapt.

When adaptation isn't possible or acceptable, it's time to take action. What routines can you shake up? What experiments can you and your teammates try? What alternative solutions might there be? Act, act, act.

Acting lets you take control of your attitude, work, and decisions, whereas adapting asks you to relinquish control of what you create or what it takes to get there. The trick is knowing what you can actually control and when to do it.

"The closest to being in control we'll ever be is in that moment when we realize we're not."

—Brian Kessler, toy designer and inventor

## Control is a hit of certainty in an uncertain world.

Control is a natural response to the inevitable uncertainty, riskiness, and messiness of collaboration and creativity. Telling others what to do, insisting things must happen one way, isolating yourself so others can't interfere with what you're doing, fighting to fit everything into a framework—these are examples of grasping for control. It's one of our natural instincts: looking for a safe place, somewhere that is known and comfortable and predictable. Control can get in the way of a culture of exploration and cocreation. If you can let go of an unhealthy need and instead achieve a dynamic "take/release" relationship with control, you get to something better: trust.

> "Teams can only handle ambiguity if there's high trust."
>
> —Suzanne Gibbs Howard, dean of IDEO U

## Trust is greater than control.

This idea of trust might sound ~~terrible to control freaks~~ hard—because it is. When you're inundated with unknowns, uncertainties, and ambiguity, it's easy to lose trust in those around you and in your own ability to make decisions and respond. When you're trusting of yourself and others, you're open. You're letting go of expectations. You're able to be empathetic. You act and adapt, despite unknowns. And each time you trust, you create more trust and, ultimately, confidence.

In the next chapters, we share a set of tools to increase your ability to act and adapt in the face of the unknown to gain greater trust—in yourself and others.

Building these mindsets and practices into strong skills over time may sound like a somewhat daunting endeavor. If you're really on the hunt for a quick fix or immediate solution here, we can tell you from experience that the real secret to building an ability to act and adapt is

"It's like driving a car at night. You never see further than your headlights, but you can make the whole trip that way."

—E. L. Doctorow

## Navigating ambiguity is a balancing act.

Acting and adapting. Trust and control. Fast and slow. Big and small. Clarity and obscurity.

Rigidly fixating on one static tactic or expecting the same strategy to work every time is antithetical to ambiguity. When you're in balance, you're in a state where opposing forces are in harmony. Continual adjustments keep you upright. You are toggling and holding tensions. It's an active thing, like a dance.

Design thrives on tensions. If you let conflicting ideas coexist, you create fertile ground for opportunity. The creative space *between* this and that allows you to bend and respond to the possibilities that come your way. Holding two (sometimes seemingly opposite) ideas at the same time gets you thinking beyond the binary, beyond *this* or *that*.

As you go through the "balances," you'll notice some contradictions. Sometimes we will tell you to do one thing, other times the exact opposite. And that's kind of the point.

No single tactic works all the time, and a tactic that works well now might be kryptonite later. What you choose to do is context-dependent. Mix and match and blend and dial to get where you need to go. Enjoy the contradictions, and pay attention to what works for you and when.

## These balances give you an infinite toolbox.

Every person, industry, and society has their preferred tools and methodologies for wayfinding across different environments, from ocean to desert to sky. Similarly, you will have your individual toolbox for different challenges—from managing the stress of the unknown to sparking creativity.

When a tool is a dynamic continuum, you get an infinite toolbox. Combine, slide, scale, and adjust. Try things out. Take the time to reflect. Take time to adapt things. Learn what works for you (and what doesn't). Discard old tools. Invent new ones. There isn't a finite thing to attain or master. Rather, you are amassing an infinite navigating ambiguity toolkit, born of your own abilities, preferences, needs, and progress.

# Five things to balance when navigating ambiguity:

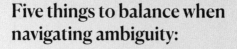

Look In • Look Out
**balance your perspective**

Speed Up • Slow Down
**balance your pace**

Focus • Unfocus
**balance your attention**

Follow the Course • Create Your Own Path
**balance your process**

Zoom In • Zoom Out
**balance your scale**

**Look In**

**Look Out**

**A week into his year at the d.school**, Civic Innovation Project Fellow Chris Rudd had a panicked look. His project, Expunge.io—a free service in Illinois that guides anyone with a juvenile record through the process of expunging their criminal record—was accepted, accelerated, and launched by the State of California. It was swept out of his hands and into action (a great problem to have, but still). Chris had to find another project, and fast.

Chris turned to his other fellows and admitted, "I'm lost. I have no idea what my project is now. I'm freaking out." Their response? "Uh, yeah. We're lost and freaking out, too." This little acknowledgment unlocked something for Chris. His fellowship was full of ambiguity. But his openness about his discomfort lightened the situation and ignited connection. When he was feeling lost, turning to others with honesty helped him get out of his head and open up to new ideas of what his next steps might be.

His colleagues suggested he create the project that was true to his values, not what he thought others would want him to do. He knew he believed in the power of technology as a tool for social change, and he wanted to increase the number of Black and Brown youth entering higher education with technical majors. This wasn't the complete picture yet, but it was a start.

When confronted with ambiguity, look in. Check in with yourself. Creative work is personal and fed by your beliefs and convictions about what matters. Learn how ambiguity makes you feel, set boundaries, and give yourself the same support you would want from others.

Once you have your own oxygen mask on, look out. Recognize where others are with ambiguity, and support them however you can. All creative work is influenced—and made better— by the people, context, and environment around you. Don't pressure yourself to come up with all the answers.

In the end, it worked out for Chris. He went on to design Youth Tech Design, a program that puts students in the driver's seat to design, build, and launch new tech solutions. But his initial freak-out was a big inspiration to the d.school's work on navigating ambiguity. So thank you for that, Chris.

# Look in.

### Notice the signs for yourself.

What happens in your body when you experience the unknown? Some physical responses to ambiguity might include (but aren't limited to) confusing dreams, night sweats, head scratching, racing heart rate, buying crystals, nail biting, angst, ennui, or even malaise. Do any of these ring a bell?

> "Find out who you are and do it on purpose."
>
> —Dolly Parton

True self-awareness means recognizing the patterns in your emotions and behavior. Equestrian leadership coach Jude Jennison puts it this way: "Your learning and growth start with self-awareness." Then, and only then, can you begin to do something about it.

### Turning on your self-awareness is easier said than done.

Our response to ambiguity—both our interpretations and our emotional response—is not objective. It's deeply connected to experience, context, history, and character. As Jennison describes, past pain and trauma are closer to the surface when we confront ambiguity, and it is much easier to be triggered by little things—like someone interrupting you to ask a question, or taking too long to respond, or playing music so loud through their headphones that you think you might walk over there right now and grab their headphones and throw them into the sea.

The process of knowing yourself is a lifelong journey. It's a marathon, not a sprint. Your situational best is still your best.

Just as ambiguity describes being open to more than one interpretation, there is no one "right" way to respond. How you deal with ambiguity—in a team and alone—is up to you. There's no one right interpretation, and that's something to celebrate.

## Find courage in your convictions.

At the d.school, we really challenge students to be laser-focused on the people they're designing for first. But that doesn't mean their personal point of view can't be part of the equation. Your unique values and perspectives can propel your work forward when faced with the unknown and can also provide an anchor when your project (invariably) takes a turn.

Designer Kelly Schmutte loved ballet from an early age and was curious to see if she could improve the (often painful) experience of dancing on pointe. But her early designs for customized footwear were met with skepticism and outright resistance by many fitters, teachers, and elite studios. In a world as conservative as classical ballet, she saw that change would not come quickly. A deep conviction that dancers deserved better sustained her work through years of shut doors and failed prototypes. With time, she figured out a way to adapt the classic pointe shoe by designing a simple method for dancers to make their own customized shoe inserts. Using moldable silicone putty that fills the spaces inside the toe area and provides more even support, dancers can prevent painful pressure buildup and protect their feet over the long run. When social media platforms offered a new way to connect directly with professional dancers, Kelly and her business PerfectFit Pointe got a lucky break. Over the course of ten years, her purpose-fueled persistence had paid off, growing into a successful business that now provides relief to dancers' toes around the world.

**Here are a few ways to look inward and get in touch with your internal sources of motivation.**

## Declare a mission (or two).

Sometimes it helps to write your focus down on paper. Try the simple structure of "I'm working on _____ in order to _____ because _____." Take a couple of stabs at it. Share it with your partners, friends, or team. What rings true when you read it out loud? What sounds amiss?

## Look for purposeful intersections.

Make three lists: "needs in the world that move me/us," "my/our skills and abilities," and "things I/we love." Then use these to populate a Venn diagram. What projects are you already working on that live at the intersection? Or if you selected one thing at random from each of the three circles, what new project could you generate that would combine all three?

### Ask "why?" and "how?" to shape a cone of possibility.

Understand your motivations in order to diversify your destinations. By repeatedly asking "why?" you can figure out where you really want to go, and by repeatedly asking "how?" you can find more ways to get there.

**Try this:**

- Write down a current goal in the middle of a piece of paper. Draw three to five lines above it. On the first line above your goal, write down *why* you want to achieve that goal. Keep asking *why* to level up several more times.

- How do you feel about your whys? Do they make you proud? Are they yours, or are they really for someone else?

- Pick a why that feels true. Ask yourself how else you could explore or satisfy that why. Get more specific as you go down. One of them will be your original starting goal, but there will be many others as you begin to flesh out a "cone of possibility." Do you see alternatives to your current goal that you like more?

# Look out.

### Navigating ambiguity is a team sport.

You would never dive to the ocean floor alone—you need a full-on crew to get there. It's easier to face ambiguity together, in community with others, rather than alone. Building this kind of trust means relinquishing some control and having faith that others have your back when (not if) you fail.

As Stanford Management Science and Engineering Professor Pam Hinds notes, "Cognitive diversity is essential in reaching breakthrough ideas." People gravitate toward people like themselves because it feels easy and predictable. Opening yourself up and trusting people with different skills and views is rarely easy. Working with people unlike yourself (in terms of identity, education, income, experience, age, geography, anything) can open you to uncertainty. Nevertheless, having different perspectives makes creative problem solving better. It's often the only way to see what we can't see ourselves.

## Check in with those around you.

You might feel comfortable with the unknown, able to dive headfirst into challenges and open things up beyond current reality. But if everyone around you is struggling with ambiguity, looking at you with anxious eyes and furrowed brows, you might not get anywhere. Leadership through the unknown requires checking in with those around you to help them navigate—even, and especially, when you're feeling the weight of ambiguity too. Ask others how they're doing, even if it feels awkward. An obvious but too-seldom-used place to start is asking, "How are you feeling?" Encourage dialogue, especially when there are different perspectives to hear and learn from.

## Learn from others.

Out of every lesson to be learned from human-centered design, this one is the keystone. Designers emphasize looking out to needs beyond our own because it's a simple and effective (though often overlooked) way of getting to powerful new ideas. At the d.school, we also care deeply about coaching empathic future leaders who put others' needs before their own. This includes observing and noticing within different contexts, empathizing with people, embracing diverse viewpoints, and including them in the process.

Empathy requires us to step into someone's world. This can be vulnerable for all involved. It takes a lot of time, effort, and willingness to engage with the messy business of understanding other people, but it's worth it, because you'll discover things that many others are afraid to explore. Here are a few ways to do it . . .

## ~~Interview~~ Have a conversation.

It might seem counterintuitive or odd to talk to someone without knowing what you might learn from them. But not knowing what you'll learn is precisely the mindset you must take to open yourself up to new ways of thinking about and looking at the world. Start by talking to the people you're creating for. See the world through their eyes.

## Look.

How can you cultivate a habit of watching and noticing?
By actively practicing it. Give yourself a task to notice all
the yellow things in the room or all the signs on your street.
Try carrying a notebook with you to practice capturing
observations, quotes, sketches, and ideas. Challenge
yourself to sit quietly in one place and just soak in the
behaviors and environment around you for a period of
time that feels longer than comfortable, and you might
be surprised at what you find.

## Cultivate your curiosity.

As a designer, you need to develop an insatiable curiosity
and desire to understand. These open you up to exploring
new ideas, holding them in parallel, and finding ways to
make them work. What awakens your curiosity? Listening to
obscure New Wave music? Wandering in nature? Holing up
in a local bookstore? Writing experimental late-night poetry?
Look for ways to broaden your context outside of your work,
and you might serendipitously spark inspiration. Cultivating
creativity is a great excuse to try something new.

# How do you know when to . . .

## Look in?

When something is making
you feel icky

When the world is telling you
something and you don't agree

When you're afraid

When you're faced
with conflicting opinions

Anytime

## Look out?

When you think you're alone

When you need to check your bias

When you're devoid of inspiration
and curiosity

When you've lost connection
to others

When you're sick of looking in

**Speed Up**

Slow Down

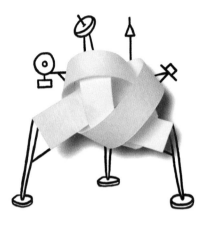

**"I believe that this nation should commit itself to**
achieving the goal, before this decade is out, of landing a
man on the moon and returning him safely to the Earth."
On May 25, 1961, President John F. Kennedy made this bold
declaration before a joint session of Congress. His vision
for building a space exploration program that could help
the United States reach this audacious goal would set the
space race in motion. Everyone involved, from pilots in
the air to engineers on the ground, would be navigating
immense ambiguity in pursuit of this literal moonshot.
NASA was entering the unknown, at rocket speed.

But, over the course of this nearly ten-year mission to the moon, NASA didn't just move fast; they had to modulate their pace every step of the way to build confidence in the mission. When public support flagged as tax dollars disappeared without seeing progress, they had to speed up. And when they worked too quickly and lost human life as a result—the Apollo 1 launch pad fire killed three astronauts—they had to slow down. Launching too fast and too soon would mean certain death. Launching too slowly would mean public failure.

When Apollo 11 finally made its lunar landing and astronaut Neil Armstrong set foot on the moon, it was a triumph for all of humankind. For NASA, managing and changing their pace of work was key to working in and with ambiguity. We'd never have gotten a person to the moon without knowing when to speed up or slow down.

Stewing in ambiguity is sometimes at odds with the "move fast, act first" experimental nature of some design approaches. Yes, sometimes moving and experimenting rapidly is precisely what you need to do to get answers and move through the unknown. But you also need patience to allow hidden possibilities to emerge. Simmering and stewing require time. Managing and changing the pace of your work is key to working with ambiguity.

# Speed up.

### Start (*before* you're ready).

Sometimes you feel like you can't get started until everything is in place (be it your skills, knowledge, finances, confidence, oven cleanliness, or whatever). "Once we're sure we can pull it off, *then* we'll get going. For destinations unknown (career change, unproven business idea, life transformation) the foolproof ten-step plan won't get us there," writes educator Matthew Trinetti. "Start once you're ready is a surefire way to never begin." One way to get started is to just do a quick experiment. Designers have an incurable itch to express something, an eager and egoless willingness to just "try it out."

You might *never* feel ready to enter the unknown, but you have to step into ambiguity and **start anyway.** Put pen to paper, type a few lines of code, stretch the canvas, dip your toe in. What can you do or make in order to help you start thinking (and not the other way around)?

### Check your judgment at the door.

The secret to quickly coming up with ideas—whether written, drawn, or built—is to relax your mind into a mode of acceptance and eliminate your natural tendency to block ideas that don't seem on point or feasible. It's a simple concept that is hard to practice. The trick is to set some limits so you don't spin out. One way to do this is to . . .

## Set an expiration date.

Parkinson's law states that work will fill the time you set aside to do it. Time management coach Elizabeth Grace Saunders suggests "deciding in advance how much time you will spend on a particular task or part of a task, and then sticking to it." For example, if you like to over-research, give yourself only until the end of the day. As the designer Charles Eames said, "The best you can do between now and Tuesday is still a kind of best you can do."

## Prioritize what you need to know (now).

It's easy to get lost in the details. Who doesn't love a good research rabbit hole? It's fun to keep learning, but beware of our friend procrastination hiding in disguise, tempting us down endless tunnels to nowhere. Try to separate out what's essential to know now versus what would be nice to know in the near future. If you have enough information to inform your next step, move on.

## Take away the hurdles.

If you're having trouble getting an undefined or difficult thing done quickly, have everything you need ready to go. For example, if you have a big project to do tomorrow, set everything up the night before, just as athletes pack their workout bag and set it next to the door. When you remove the practical (and perceived) barriers to getting started, they won't slow you down as much.

# Slow down.

### "When you feel the need to speed up, slow down."

Activist, artist, champion diver, and spearfisher Kimi Werner learned to become calm in the face of the unknown, gaining the courage to hold her breath for upward of four minutes and forty-five seconds. In her 2014 TEDxMaui talk, Kimi described her feelings like this: "So many times when something goes wrong, when fear kicks in, or when you realize how far away you are from air, it can be so natural to want to react by *speeding up*. Kicking harder, swimming faster, and trying to get back to safety sooner. But it's actually those precise moments when you should *slow down*."

Why is this the case? "Moving faster underwater takes more energy: it raises your heart rate, and you can quickly burn through all of that oxygen you have saved up from that single breath of air you took at the surface," Kimi explains. "Slowing down conserves your oxygen. It keeps your heart rate low. But most importantly, it allows you to be calm enough to see things clearly so that you can make good decisions."

This is good advice when you're diving with sharks. It works in other situations, too. The urge to speed up can be a true indicator of a need to slow down, and that might just give you the clarity you need.

### Slow down now to speed up later.

Early on, invest the time to experiment with many different ideas to get inspired. Create rough prototypes and experiments that require little effort and low cost. Use them to understand whether you're on the right track. With time and feedback, you'll home in on your approach and be able to pick up the pace with confidence.

### Percolation takes patience.

While slowing down can feel like wasted time or seem lazy, it is fertile ground for creative work. We have to make room for things to make sense and take shape.

> "Genius is eternal patience."
>
> —Michelangelo

In design, this process is referred to as synthesis, when disparate pieces of information are brought together to find insight and opportunity. It might involve looking for patterns, making leaps toward new ideas, or mapping data to uncover new possibilities. In any case, this work requires stewing, deliberation, and discussion, and patience is rewarded.

Slowing down was a critical part of the NOW Hunters Point Project, an effort to transform a former industrial landscape in San Francisco's Bayview–Hunters Point into a public activity center. Designer and spatial justice activist Liz Ogbu embraced a community-centered design approach from the very beginning. To gather input from community members, Liz and her team had to slow down. This allowed the time to hold events for individuals to share their real, beautiful, and often painful stories of Hunters Point, which was crucial for creating inclusivity and an opportunity to heal.

Often, answers and solutions come only with time. As Jude Jennison explains in her book *Leading Through Uncertainty*, "A fast-paced, high-pressure work environment is not conducive to creating *space*." Giving yourself the space, time, and permission to really observe or understand something is a key ingredient in generating creative ideas.

A great place to start calming your thoughts is by slowing down your breath.

So . . . breathe.

Or don't breathe, if you're Kimi Werner.

# How do you know when to . . .

## Speed up?

When deadlines are looming

When your idea definitely isn't ready
to show

When you're overwhelmed by options
and choice

When you're paralyzed by what's in
front of you

When your stove has never been cleaner


## Slow down?

When your heart palpitations have
become distracting

When you need time to process

When everyone is talking in circles
and not listening to each other

When things are complex or sensitive

When you feel the need to speed up

# Focus

Unfocus

**For more than five hundred years**, she has fueled conspiracy theories, provoked heated criticisms about her crowds, and inspired innumerable souvenirs with her moniker. In 1852, her image drove artist Luc Maspero to throw himself from the fourth floor of a Parisian hotel; he left a note that supposedly read, "For years I have grappled desperately with her smile. I prefer to die."

All that for Leonardo da Vinci's *Mona Lisa*, a 1'9" by 2'6" oil painting from 1503, housed in the Louvre. Journalist John Lichfield dubbed it "the most visited, written about, sung about, and parodied work of art in the world."

In *How to Think Like Leonardo da Vinci*, Michael J. Gelb writes that da Vinci painted the *Mona Lisa* using a technique called *sfumato*, resulting in forms—in the artist's own words—"without lines or borders, in the manner of smoke or beyond the focus plane." *Sfumato* directly translates from Italian as "turned to mist" or "up in smoke." It describes the dreamy, misty effect created by tiny brushstrokes and veils of paint that blur the edges of subjects in a painting. Instead of sharp, crisp lines, it is as if you're looking at it through a steamy window.

The *Mona Lisa* is a textbook example of *sfumato*, but its fame really comes from the subject's enigmatic smile. In a *New York Times* article about this smile, Sandra Blakeslee wrote, "First she is smiling. Then the smile fades. A moment later the smile returns only to disappear again. What is with this lady's face?"

We used to think the painting's compelling draw was the mystery of the woman's gaze. What was she looking at? Was she smiling at a loved one? Or a lover? Or did she just catch the eye of a friend she bailed on with the excuse that she was at a jousting tournament? Awkward.

Today, there is another, more concrete explanation. Dr. Margaret Livingstone, a Harvard neuroscientist and authority on visual processing, points out that the mysterious smile "comes and goes because of how the human visual system is designed, not because the expression is ambiguous." She says the human eye has two distinct regions for seeing the world: a peripheral area where we see black and white, motion, and shadows and a central area where we see color and pick out details.

When you look directly at Mona Lisa's eyes, her mouth is in your peripheral vision. Because your peripheral vision is more interested in shadows than details, it prioritizes the shadows from her cheekbones. These shadows are curved in a way that tells your brain she is smiling. But when you look directly at her mouth, your peripheral vision does *not* see the shadows, so you *don't* read a smile. Dr. Livingstone points out, "You'll never be able to catch her smile by looking at her mouth."

This flickering quality—serene smile there, then gone— occurs as you move your focus around Mona Lisa's face. The smile doesn't change. Your focus does.

We see things differently when we shift our focus, in more ways than one. According to Dr. Srini Pillay, a psychiatrist and brain researcher, "The brain operates optimally when it toggles between focus and unfocus," which helps build resilience and boost creativity.

Da Vinci embodies this. As Gelb writes, "This ability to embrace uncertainty by 'blurring the edges' and to hold opposites in tension was not only characteristic of his painting, but of his life." Periods of rest and work across many different disciplines allowed da Vinci to return recharged, refreshed, and ready to focus.

Both focus and unfocus are vital, and our work demands that we practice both. Being able to shift our attention in the face of uncertainty, to focus and unfocus, is a powerful secret of unleashing creative potential. Reality changes in the periphery.

# Focus.

## Spend less time on trivial stuff.

Unlimited choices and decisions are constantly demanding and depleting our attention. Making faster decisions about smaller, inconsequential things frees up our time and focus.

Easier said than done, right?

Finishing unimportant tasks is just so *rewarding*. For example, you might need to work on your portfolio, but before you know it, you've spent an hour rewriting your biography or Googling different types of Poodle mixes. There's probably a live stream of Golden Doodle puppies somewhere on the internet *right now*.

Hey! *snap snap* Eyes back on the page.

As writer and emotions expert Dr. Alice Boyes points out, "Unimportant tasks have a nasty tendency of taking up more time than they should." We give them more attention, too. According to a study conducted by Meng Zhu, Yang Yang, and Christopher K. Hsee in 2018, people tend to complete *urgent tasks* (which they define as "tasks with short completion windows" and "more immediate and certain payoffs") over *important tasks* ("tasks with larger outcomes" and "further away goals"). This means low-importance, time-specific tasks (like doing invoices or rearranging your sticky notes by size and color) get done, but you still haven't pursued bigger, more nebulous goals (like changing careers or tackling your crippling phobia of improv).

Focus is crucial to navigating ambiguity because it keeps you steady in the face of the unknown. It is easy to get distracted and overcome by the multitudes of decisions and possibilities out there. Limit yourself to making the most important moves, or give yourself a time limit for how long you'll spend in la-la-land. Do what you need to do (within reason) to protect your focus.

## If you're on, be on.

Decide what your primo focus moments are, make them realistic, and stick to them. In the moment, intense active focus can be downright exhausting and un-fun, but it feels so good afterward. Think about it: you wouldn't show up at the gym for a workout class, only to step out for thirty minutes to take a casual call with a friend.

## Set up a parking lot for ideas and questions.

Don't squelch rogue flashes of inspiration that come up when you're focused. Stash them in a project parking lot so you can revisit them later. Dedicate a specific place for these to make sure you capture them without slowing momentum.

## Make mini-decisions.

It is sometimes easier to make a series of small decisions instead of one big "perfect" decision. Don't overload a given decision with too much importance. Instead, break it down into smaller next steps. Checking off a few of those smaller tasks might be enough to build momentum and get you unstuck. What's a smaller next step you can take? What can you do to test your idea in ten minutes? What is the thing blocking you the most?

### Get matching headbands for your team.

It might seem silly, but a simple physical artifact can act as a reminder to stay present and work together. Who doesn't love matching neon yellow sweatbands? (Trust us—they work.)

# Unfocus.

### There's an upside of downtime.

As you might recall, Dr. Margaret Livingstone had an epiphany about that *Mona Lisa* smile. This epiphany didn't occur while she was in front of the painting; it occurred on her bike ride home from the museum. This kind of thing comes up a lot—creative people seem to land on their best ideas in random places, like in the shower or while staring at a lava lamp.

Many companies seek to build a culture of "nonstop innovation," but innovation comes only with a healthy dose of *unfocusing* from our overly scheduled work and lives.

Unfocusing is different from being distracted. Your brain needs a "break," but it's still working to solve problems. Some of our most creative ideas come from this very intentional but ambiguous place.

## Do mostly nothing.

Dr. Srini Pillay says, "When you unfocus, you engage a brain circuit called the 'default mode network,'" or DMN. He reports that this circuit uses a whopping 20 percent of our body's energy, whereas intense concentration (like doing a calculus problem or reading Simone de Beauvoir) requires only an additional 5 percent. "The DMN needs this energy because it is doing anything but resting. Under the brain's conscious radar, it activates old memories, goes back and forth between the past, present, and future, and recombines different ideas."

Pillay says that a great mnemonic for remembering the DMN is "Do Mostly Nothing." To clarify slightly, doing mostly nothing usually means doing a little something else. This might be driving, watching water boil, petting an animal, swinging, pushing someone on a swing, people-watching, going for a run, looking at art, anything that doesn't push your brain too hard. Scrub the oven. Tidy your desk. Paint a wall. Allow your mind to wander away from the thing you're trying to solve.

## Give yourself a break.

Gelb describes how when Leonardo da Vinci was creating *The Last Supper*, he would spend days at a time on a scaffold, painting nonstop all day. Then suddenly, without warning, he would disappear for half a day or longer. Da Vinci learned to follow a rhythm of intense focus and relaxation to maximize his creativity. He was fueled by sharing and discussing ideas with others, but he also needed solo time for creative insights to come. In his *Treatise on Painting*, da Vinci wrote, "It is well that you should often leave off work and take a little relaxation because when you come back you are a better judge." When we remove cerebral congestion with a little downtime, we naturally restore the brain's attention, motivation, productivity, creativity, and performance.

## Call it something that reflects its value.

What language do you use when you talk about unfocused time? Do you call it a "break" or an "energy boost"? The way you refer to it could help you make your case for yourself and for your organization.

> "Let it be still, and it will gradually become clear."
>
> —Lao Tzu, *Tao Te Ching*

### End the day with a question or idea.

Rather than planning to end the day with a certain deliverable, which provides a nice sense of closure and completeness, try ending the day with questions. For a few minutes before going to bed, think about the thing you are trying to solve. Let go of expectations, and let those questions simmer while you sleep.

### Stop reading this book.

Yep, you. Go outside! Go play with a kitten! Go listen to some music! (Other than Steely Dan.) Nah, just kidding; listen to all the Steely Dan you want! Go for a run! Go knit a scarf! Just *go*. Your brain will thank you. But please come back.

# How do you know when to . . .

## Focus?

When there are a thousand
decisions to be made

When your work requires more
brain juice than usual

When you're nearing the metaphorical end

When distractions abound. Look, a bunny!

When you can't stop saying, "You know
what else would be cool?"

## Unfocus?

When you've been staring at a
screen for too long

When you can't remember the
last time you moved your body

When you've read the same thing
thirty times

When muscling through isn't working

When you've tried everything else

Follow the Course

Create Your Own Path

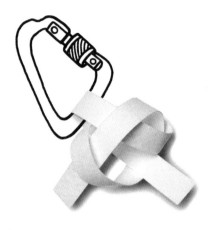

**Trails have proven to be** a pretty useful invention throughout human history. They show you where to go, and they bring you back to where you started. They keep nature safe, and they keep you safe. They keep you from getting lost. Trail systems go across, over, under, and even up. Straight up.

El Capitan, the giant granite monolith looking down with commanding presence over Yosemite Valley, was once considered unclimbable. Today, with well over sixty established routes, it sets the standard for big wall climbing and has been summited by hundreds of climbers, from ten-year-old Selah Schneiter to eighty-one-year-old Gary Bloch.

Following established routes up the soaring three-thousand-foot stone face allows climbers to practice, improve, and compare their performance. On June 3, 2017, Alex Honnold became the first person to free-solo El Cap—climbing the wall with no ropes, no harness, no gear, nothing at all. Just him, his shoes, a bag of chalk, and the wall.

Alex planned his climb following the Freerider route, considered the "easiest" and most popular for free climbing El Cap. Free climbing involves using ropes and other equipment only as protection against falls, not as an aid in the ascent. He rehearsed and perfected the climb (with ropes) for more than six weeks until he could visualize every step in his head before attempting the real deal. When he made the ascent—with minor route modifications and *no* ropes—in a breezy three hours and fifty-six minutes, it was a triumph for the sport (and a huge sigh of relief for the camera crew and everyone else in his life). He was able to do something once considered impossible, made possible by the many climbers who had charted and practiced the route before him.

Charting new routes can break the boundaries of human achievement and allow us to experience things never before seen or felt by other people. Long before Alex came along, people weren't sure El Cap could be free climbed at all.

The most visually striking part of the rock is called "The Nose," a massive prow formed by the joining of its two primary faces. Lynn Hill became the first person (and first woman) ever to free climb The Nose in 1993 over the course of four days. One particular pitch that had stopped many before her is called "Changing Corners" (graded 5.14a/b—nearly at the top of the climbing difficulty scale), which is now considered the technical crux of the climb. With virtually no holds and a 90-degree corner jutting out from the wall, it required extreme creativity, persistence, and athleticism for Lynn to work past this formation. And only a year later, she bested her own record with a time of twenty-three hours, cementing her climbs on The Nose as some of the most impressive in climbing history.

But perhaps the biggest impact of Lynn's achievement was how it reshaped the sport's understanding of what it means (and looks like) to be an elite climber, particularly relative to physical characteristics. She explained, "If a lot of good climbers have come and tried to do it and failed, and a woman comes and does it first, it's really meaningful." She's credited with bringing many more female climbers to a largely male-dominated sport.

Creating your own path can pave the way for others—and inspire others to seek out their own paths. Following the course can lead you to greater heights in different ways. The route to your destination is yours to climb (or walk— we're taking the trail, too).

# Follow the course.

## Maps give us (and our fellow travelers) confidence.

In times of great uncertainty, it can be reassuring to revisit tried and true frameworks and processes. Process maps or diagrams, however oversimplified they might be, can make a creative process feel structured, contained, and tidy. This can bring a sense of calm and order to something that feels very intangible and messy. Maps and diagrams have often emerged and evolved from years of experience and can neatly package a lot of cultural wisdom.

Kathryn Segovia, the d.school's head of Learning Experience Design for Executive Education, uses process to orient learners. "Anytime we teach someone new to design thinking, we give them a roadmap in the form of a process," she says. "We use this map almost like training wheels. Innovation work is *messy* and it can feel very uncomfortable. A process map can help new learners develop enough initial confidence in this uncertain work that they are willing to continue and push onward."

Frameworks are a great starting point. You don't always have to reinvent the wheel. Designers use structured processes all the time to develop new products and solve problems. There are tools aplenty for learning from others, synthesizing information, prototyping, and so on. Look around you to see what kinds of trusted tools, methods, and processes are available for your creative endeavors. Someone has almost always gone there before you. Get their map if you can.

## Maps help you communicate clearly.

A map can also help you communicate with others and demystify your process. If you're planning on going on a hike, and you tell your family the specific trailhead you're starting at and how long you expect to be gone, they feel some degree of safety regarding your whereabouts. But if you casually say, "I'm headed out for an adventure in the desert!" (or even worse, leave no note at all), you're going to cause alarm. A map helps you communicate the essentials of your planned excursion (even if in reality you anticipate deviating from it).

## Maps make the journey clearer for everyone.

We've already said that navigating ambiguity is a team sport, so if you have a team, having everyone be authentically included is a big deal. As d.school cofounder David Kelley says, "Sometimes the details of the process don't matter as much as having a clear process that everyone agrees to." That might be an overstatement, but the point rings true—choosing a path gets you on your way. The sense of structure that a starting process provides can help a team quickly get aligned and headed in the same direction.

If you haven't done so already, try visualizing your creative process in diagram form. Map your steps for the last five projects you did. What patterns do you see? How does your process differ from other people's?

# Create your own path.

## The recipe is ambiguous.

When you're making pancakes for the first time, the recipe on the pancake mix box is a perfect starting place. It's all laid out right there: ingredients, steps, amounts, tools, temperatures. For a first-timer, a recipe is invaluable, but it doesn't always equal success. The cooking can still result in inedible hockey pucks.

Over time and with practice, a recipe becomes so familiar that you don't really need to read it anymore. You learn to add more liquid if the batter is too viscous—or flour if it's too runny. You might play around with what you have in the pantry, adding walnuts or bananas. You might even get inspired by other people's recipes and try them at home— like the white chocolate chip macadamia nut pancakes with chantilly cream and coconut syrup you enjoyed at Maui's Gazebo Restaurant while you watched sea turtles playing in the surf, for example.

One of our students, Garth Edwards, wrote that navigating ambiguity is like "being put in a random stranger's house and being told to cook them dinner." You don't know if they're vegan, vegetarian, nut free, or religiously anti-coconut. You don't know what's in their fridge, where their utensils are, or how their stove works—and at the end of it all, they probably wanted a veggie burrito instead of beef stroganoff.

## When you're first learning to cook, a recipe is a helpful guide.

At the d.school, we help people unlock their creative potential and apply it in the world. A big part of our role is orienting students with frameworks for a process. While we've developed and used many different frameworks over the years, we don't believe there is one "right" way to go about solving problems, like having one "right" pancake recipe. "The order and process of a recipe helps new cooks get started," says Carissa Carter, the d.school's director of Teaching and Learning, "but it's only with practice, inventiveness, experimentation, and constraints that you might begin to call yourself a chef." (She introduced us to this recipe metaphor, so we trust her.)

## Design your work.

As beloved Stanford art professor, Matt Kahn, used to say, "Use design to design." By this, he meant that you should pay as much attention to *how* you create as you do to *what* you make. It might require you to start in a different place than you thought, let someone else take control for a bit, or find a new way to do an old thing. And there's no way around it: designing your work takes more effort, but it always pays off.

The Teaching and Learning Team at the d.school celebrates how educators "use design to design" at their annual Artifact Week. Teaching teams share experimental pieces of curriculum or a first prototype of new content, giving everyone in the teaching community a chance to glimpse other teams' methods. This reinforces a culture of learning where the process is just as important as the outcome.

## Respond to what's needed at the moment.

The folks at Civilla, a nonprofit civic design studio in Detroit, have plenty of experience designing their work. In 2015, they partnered with the government of Michigan to design a "faster, simpler, and more humane way for residents to apply for public assistance programs like food and healthcare." Their team paid special attention to *how* they collaborated with government leaders along the way. When they needed administrators to understand how residents experience the application, Civilla shared a gallery of stories from actual applicants and brought in residents to join the work. Both practices are reliable design approaches, but Civilla also had to improvise new ways of working when it came to testing their ideas. The complexity of 1,726 local, state, and national regulations made it nearly impossible to use their usual tactics. At that point, they had to redesign how they work.

Civilla Cofounder and COO Adam Selzer says, "It helps to have a strong understanding of defined methods . . . while being able to call on our own creativity to respond to whatever the moment requires." They followed the course *and* created their own path.

When the new application rolled out across the state in 2018, Civilla had streamlined access to assistance for 2.5 million Michigan residents. The new version is 80 percent shorter and takes only about half the time to process.

Creative work calls for constant listening and calibrating: Are you getting too enamored with one idea? Are you hearing the same things over and over? Are you doing too much talking versus doing? We ask ourselves routinely, "What does our project need right *now*?"

Miles Davis used to tell his musicians, "Don't play what's there; play what's not there." This willingness to leave room for opportunity is at the core of the art of improvisation. Given your own abilities and your sense of what your work needs, how do you adapt and respond?

# How do you know when to ...

## Follow the course?

When you're unsure of the right path forward

When time's a-wastin'

At the start

At the finish

When you're trying to achieve
the same thing the last person did

When others need to meet you or
join up with you

When it's working

## Create your own path?

When you're not getting anywhere

When you keep ending up in the same exact place

When you want to see what's behind that big tree

When the path is too small for everyone

When the path is too crowded

When the path is making you weary

When the path ends (but you haven't
arrived yet)

**Zoom In**

**Zoom Out**

**The 1977 documentary *Powers of Ten* by** designers
Ray and Charles Eames is one of the most famous short
films ever made.

The movie starts at a lakeside picnic. The camera
viewpoint is directly overhead and shows a scene one
meter wide. The camera zooms out. Every ten seconds, it
reveals a greater view, each one power of ten wider than
the last. First we see the park, then the lake, then the city,
the state, the country, and the planet, and so on, until our
galaxy is just a speck of light.

Then the camera zooms back in at the same pace. With
the picnic back in view, the camera focuses on one of the
picnicker's hands and begins to zoom closer, into the skin
texture and structure, individual cells, and so on. Now,

every ten seconds, what you see is magnified by a negative power of ten. Before you know it, you're seeing inside a proton. That's where the journey ends.

This little movie had a big impact on how science is shared. By moving between the tiny details of molecular biology to the enormous expanses of astrophysics, the film reveals interconnections across scientific fields. Comprehending scale, or as the Eameses liked to call it, "the effect of adding another zero," helps connect these hidden dots, making us better designers—and citizens.

Eames Demetrios, grandson of Ray and Charles, believes scale is a timeless method for navigating ambiguity: "Many of the challenges we are facing today are a combination of things very big with opportunities and threats and things very small that have opportunities and threats." And you can't really navigate these big opportunities unless you understand the basics: What are you dealing with? How big is it? What is its relationship to other things? Whether it's a weird object you picked up in the attic or an abstract concept you can't let go of, "having a sense of scale," Demetrios says, "gives you tools for a new kind of understanding."

# Zoom in.

### Get into the details and knowns.

When you're shrouded in uncertainty, naming what you *do* know can get you started on making sense of a thing. Designers do product breakdowns to get a closer look at the guts of an object. Doctors take X-rays to look at the hard inner structures of the body and MRIs and PET scans to see soft tissue with more detail. Project managers use to-do lists, timetables, and calendars.

When you don't know how something works, take it apart (metaphorically or literally) and look at it closely. Ground yourself in what you know about the challenge. This can help you make connections that aren't already in your head—and create the room to explore.

### Keep it human-centered.

There's a reason *Powers of Ten* starts at the scale of humans. Connecting to the needs you want to satisfy keeps you laser-focused on the "why" behind your work. A strong point-of-view statement can be a tool for crisply defining what you're trying to navigate, who it's for, and why it matters. It can sustain motivation when you feel like you're spinning your wheels or getting stuck in the trenches. By zooming in and looking at a problem through the lens of a specific person, your work becomes more focused.

## Stick to constraints.

We deal with constraints all the time. Your kid refuses to eat carrots, you have to use a certain software, there's a deadly pandemic outside and you can't leave the house— whether known or unforeseen, constraints can feel like roadblocks. But they're often the most powerful force behind getting us to come up with creative solutions. Your greatest ideas might emerge when you have to improvise within a theme, sneakily substituting parsnips for carrots. Time, materials, budgets, space, human resources—all of these can be hugely valuable constraints. If you find yourself stuck for how to get started, you might be surprised by how zooming in on the knowns can spark a next move.

## Fall back on rules.

Stake out some "knowns" where you can, so you can feel safe to explore. Define what you need, and commit to it. On a team, sharing individual needs and outlining a common agreement on how you'll work creates a framework that can become a safety net when you're feeling unsure. For example, what times are sacred meeting times? Who is in charge of what? How will you deal with conflict? What are your communication norms?

One way to establish knowns is to create a work-back calendar. Start with your big end goal, and then work backwards in time to map out what's needed to reach your milestones.

# Zoom out.

In 1971, Edgar Mitchell was a lunar module pilot aboard
NASA's Apollo 14 mission. Mitchell was responsible for the
lunar module itself as well as science on the moon (which
is about $10^8$ meters from Earth, for those still counting).
With his jobs complete, he had a minute to kick back, so
to speak, on the return trip to Earth. And like anyone on
a bus or in a plane or on a ship, he looked out the window.
Mitchell saw the Earth—blue, bright, with a thin shell of
atmosphere surrounding it—floating in inky darkness. "In
outer space, you develop an instant global consciousness,
a people orientation, an intense dissatisfaction with the
state of the world, and a compulsion to do something
about it," Mitchell said.

This sensation is called the "overview effect," a term
coined by the philosopher Frank White. "Anyone living
in a space settlement . . . will always have an overview,"
White observed. "They will see things that we know,
but that we don't experience, which is that the Earth is
one system. We're all part of that system, and there is a
certain unity and coherence to it all."

Another NASA astronaut, Ron Garan, has focused his
career on spreading the word about the overview effect.
He believes that what he terms an "orbital perspective"
can have "profound, positive effects on the trajectory of

our global society and our world." His new mission is to "communicate the transformative power of acquiring a big picture and long-term perspective of our planet."

Designers recognize—and are energized by—the reality that everything is connected. When you're creating a new idea, it helps to move fluidly between concrete details and more abstract systems. Activities like populating a stakeholder map or visualizing the connections in a system help you zoom out to understand the full landscape of implications.

From Buckminster Fuller to Carl Sagan, people have found inspiration and insight in the concept of zooming out. When we step back and look at the big picture, we gain an intangible understanding of how things work and connect. We need to take that time to step back, reflect, and look at our world as a tiny speck. Seeing something from afar helps us understand it.

"We shall not cease from exploration, and the end of all our exploring will be to arrive where we started and know the place for the first time."

—T. S. Eliot

# How do you know when to . . .

## Zoom in?

When a detail will make
or break everything

When you're all over the map

When you've talked about an
idea only as a concept

When you've been in outer space

When you don't know how
something works

## Zoom out?

When you've been pushing pixels

When you haven't spent time looking
at the bigger picture or system

When the details just don't fit

When you need to remember what
it's all about

When you can't answer "Why are
we doing this?"

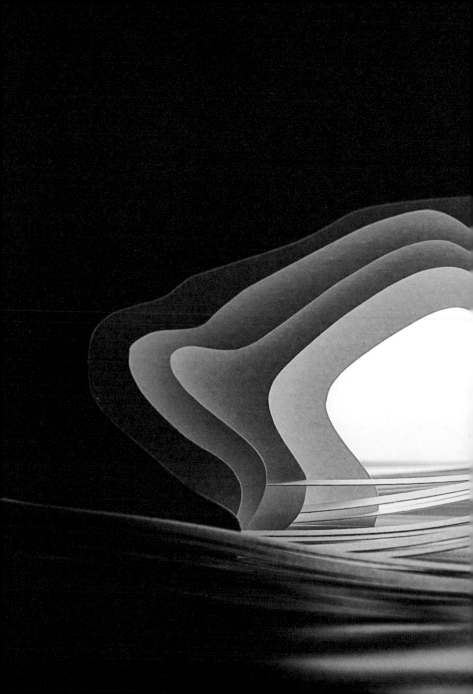

Emerge

# Ambiguity is forever, but this book is not.

### Ambiguity is a given.

We're lobbying to get it added next to death and taxes. But unlike that fun pair, when viewed a certain way, **ambiguity is also an opportunity**. For those who pause to explore, discovery awaits.

### Build your stamina.

Every ambiguous project or problem that you attempt to work through will help you in the future. But don't attempt a marathon on your first run—you'll injure yourself and probably freak out the people around you. Embracing ambiguity is an endurance sport, not a sprint. Experienced marathoners know what their body will feel like at mile 22—and how to keep pushing through it—because they've been there before. Start slowly, with a few low-risk experiments. The more you experiment and learn from your experiences, the better equipped you will be to make decisions in the future.

### Do the harder thing.

In her days as a teaching fellow, d.school Executive Director Sarah Stein Greenberg was advising a student team that had come to an impasse in a project to design a low-cost infant incubator for trained clinicians to use in urban hospitals in Nepal. The team was feeling the tension between wanting to do something they thought they could accomplish by following the design brief or going for a more complex challenge well outside of their comfort zone. They needed to create a design solution for a rural parent unable to get to a hospital when trying to save their baby in a desperate situation. Sarah says this is common with students: "They have all the raw materials they need to do something really unique, but they don't recognize its potential . . . or fear causes them to revert to a more familiar (less ambiguous!) territory."

Do they pick the route that has a clear, winnable outcome? Or do they go for the scarier, amorphous challenge? When the team asked Sarah to weigh in, she advised them to "do the thing that seems harder." The result was the design of a life-saving device: the Embrace baby incubator, which uses wax pouches (warmed in boiling water) in a sleeping-bag-like wrap to maintain a constant temperature, all for twenty-five dollars.

We know our brain wants to play it safe. If you're hemming and hawing, debating and weighing, try doing the thing that seems harder. When you lean into the thing that seems less comfortable, you may get to more interesting ideas.

## And . . . know your boundaries.

This is the corollary to doing the harder thing. Discomfort can help you learn, but too much discomfort can put you in the panic zone. All your energy gets used up in managing your anxiety, and that leaves no room for learning.

One way to recharge is by spending time in your comfort zone. If you're feeling walloped by a dip into the panic zone, recharge and build your confidence by doing what you already know and have done before. Soon you'll be ready to venture into the learning zone again.

### Working with ambiguity is about balance.

Being good at navigating ambiguity isn't a black box of mystery, but it *is* a continual exercise in awareness and decision making. When you've embarked on a voyage, you can't snooze for ten hours and expect your boat to stay the course. Navigating ambiguity requires **action**—taking purposeful initiative—and **adaptation**—flexing with changing conditions. There's a push-pull interaction between these complementary forces, between where you're going and how you're getting there. When balanced well, like peanut butter and jelly, action and adaptation will fuel your confidence (or fill your tummy) and build trust. Trust is ultimately way more powerful than control when you're up against the unknown.

### Just remember to keep moving—moving helps you balance.

If you're balancing, you might fall every now and then. If you're falling, chances are your balancing act has become too chaotic or too static. Movement doesn't have to be big to be effective. It's the motion that counts. Don't forget to pat yourself on the back for being brave enough to get on the ride, and, to further mix the metaphors, keep paddling.

**The unknown can be a scary place.** Even the familiar becomes foreboding in darkness—your local pool, the ocean, a favorite lake, the bathtub. Sharks magically materialize in the water at night. Sun's up: totally safe. Sun's down: demon creatures lurk in the deep. It's hard to trust what you can't see. It's shadowy. It's frightening. There's probably something slimy that's going to touch your foot.

Limiting beliefs might keep us comfortably on the shore or side of the pool, but they hold us back from experiencing the joys of night swimming. The exhilaration. The apprehension. The peace. The reward of giving in to something you can't fully see—and living to tell the tale.

Our collective relationship with ambiguity is becoming more defined *and* complex as we swim into unknowns together on a global scale. School, work, home, family, friends . . . *everything* in our lives has been inundated with unknowns, and it's perpetually unfolding. It's like night swimming is just life now.

We consider ourselves intermediate-novices on the topic of ambiguity, and we are proud to admit it's still uncomfortable. Sometimes it feels like we're slogging through a bog, trying to hit a moving target, or cutting cubes out of fog. In the end, we're still ~~masochists~~ advocates. We love ambiguity for the possibility it creates.

As you reenter the world after this ambiguous trip, you might not know where you're going from here. But you have everything you need to navigate there.

"I wanted a perfect ending. Now I've learned, the hard way, that some poems don't rhyme, and some stories don't have a clear beginning, middle, and end. Life is about not knowing, having to change, taking the moment and making the best of it, without knowing what's going to happen next. Delicious Ambiguity."

—Gilda Radner

# Acknowledgments

**Together, we want to (unambiguously!) thank those who have paved the way for this book by boldly exploring ambiguity at the d.school:** Dr. Hannah Jones and Nihir Shah, who also originated this work; Carissa Carter, our long-con creative catalyst; Sarah Stein Greenberg; Emily Callaghan; Mark Grundberg; and Seamus Yu Harte; and many more.

Scott Doorley and Charlotte Burgess-Auburn: Thank you for being our river guides and for truly navigating ambiguity with us. Reina Takahashi: How did we ever get so lucky as to have you as an artistic collaborator? And Andria Lo: Thank you for transforming 3D artwork into gorgeous images on the page.

To Kim Keller, Emma Campion, Mari Gill, Kristi Hein, Jane Chinn, and the whole TSP team: our thanks for your sustained efforts to make everything shine, and for solving all the unknowns on a book about ambiguity.

**From Andrea Small:** Thank you, Lauren, Jm, and Dan, for contributing with love and (usually) without context. Thank you to Melissa, Kris, Suejin, and Jade, for walking with me; and to Carrie, Chelsea, Kristen, and John, my team of medical professionals and artists. Thank you to Kelly, for diligently representing the voice of students and educators. And thank you to my mother, who always said I should write a book. For the first time, I'll admit you were right.

**From Kelly Schmutte:** To my parents and sister, thank you for creating space for wild ideas to take root and loving me no matter what. To Andrew, thank you for being my rock throughout this process and for always being my creative partner in crime. And thank you to Andrea for making this book more than twice as good as it could have been if written from only one voice.

# Sources

For a list of sources and suggested reading materials, please visit: dschool.stanford.edu/books/navigatingambiguity

# Index

Copyright © 2022 by The Board of Trustees of the Leland Stanford Junior University
on behalf of Hasso Plattner Institute of Design
Paper artwork copyright © 2022 by Reina Takahashi
Photographs copyright © 2022 by Andria Lo

Line drawings by Kelly Schmutte and Andrea Small
Additional photographs on pages iv–v, 29, 40–41 by Scott Doorley

Library of Congress Cataloging-in-Publication Data
Names: Small, Andrea, author. | Schmutte, Kelly, author.
Title: Navigating ambiguity: creating opportunity in a world of unknowns /
    by Andrea Small and Kelly Schmutte, Stanford d.school.
Description: First edition. | California: Ten Speed Press, 2022.
Identifiers: LCCN 2020032125 (print) | LCCN 2020032126 (ebook) |
    ISBN 9781984857965 (trade paperback) | ISBN 9781984857972 (ebook)
Subjects: LCSH: Creative ability. | Design. | Ambiguity.
Classification: LCC BF408.S483 2021 (print) | LCC BF408 (ebook) |
    DDC 153.3/5—dc23
LC record available at https://lccn.loc.gov/2020032125
LC ebook record available at https://lccn.loc.gov/2020032126

Trade Paperback ISBN: 978-1-9848-5796-5
eBook ISBN: 978-1-9848-5797-2

Printed in China

Acquiring editor: Hannah Rahill | Editor: Kim Keller
Art director and designer: Emma Campion | Production designer: Mari Gill
Typefaces: Hope Meng's d.sign, Commericial Type's Canela, Dinamo's Whyte,
    and DSTypes Foundry's Acta
Production and prepress color manager: Jane Chinn
Copyeditor: Kristi Hein | Proofreader: Lisa D. Brousseau | Indexer: Ken DellaPenta
Publicist: David Hawk | Marketers: Daniel Wikey and Windy Dorresteyn
d.school creative team: Charlotte Burgess-Auburn,
    Scott Doorley, and Nariman (Nadia) Gathers

10 9 8 7 6 5 4 3 2 1

First Edition